The Annual Client Review System

The Annual Client Review System

A Client Handbook

Karl N. Kindschi, LUTCF

Writer's Showcase
San Jose New York Lincoln Shanghai

The Annual Client Review System
A Client Handbook

Writer's Showcase
an imprint of iUniverse, Inc.

For information address:
iUniverse, Inc.
5220 S. 16th St., Suite 200
Lincoln, NE 68512
www.iuniverse.com

ISBN: 0-595-22254-4

Printed in the United States of America

Preface

When someone in the insurance industry writes a book, it's normally intended for agents in the insurance industry. This is not the case. This handbook is dedicated to clients. <u>My clients</u>. This handbook attempts to cover the basics of insurance planning and financial products, which sometimes simply doesn't get covered during our interviews together.

Over the last eighteen years, I have spent eight years as an insurance agent developing and working with clients. For five more years I worked both as an agent and trainer. Ninety five percent of my time then, was spent in personal production (sales) and the other five percent was spent in training other, newer agents. I left that position and spent one additional year as an Advanced Marketing Specialist on a full time basis, working with 16 other agents and their clients on their personal insurance, estate protection and business continuation cases.

Then at the corporate level I was asked to serve in the capacity of Director of Life Sales and Training with a small mutual insurance company based in Madison, Wisconsin. I served in that capacity for four years, holding four insurance licenses and three securities licenses including a Registered Principal license supervising all of the 140 Registered Representatives in the state of Wisconsin.

As a former director of a mutual insurance company, I trained insurance agents. I trained licensed agents in the areas of life insurance, disability income insurance, long term care insurance, annuities and mutual funds.

The investment and insurance industry has changed more in the last twenty years than it probably has in the last sixty. I've seen a lot of it. During the last seventeen years, I have participated in many training sessions, seminars and meetings. I've even conducted my share of them. It seems that there was, is now and will be to come, a tremendous volume of vital information, and terrific concepts to be shared.

That is why I'm writing this client handbook. This handbook is simply a collection of concepts, thoughts and ideas I've collected over the years. Some of it is original; some has been handed down to me from those who I've been associated with over the years. Some of it has come from many of my insightful clients.

This handbook is intended to give you some background on why I ask the questions that I ask of you. It includes real life examples. Some are good ones to exemplify and some examples are meant to illustrate what not to do. It simply uses true to life cases in point.

It has been said that... 'It's stupid when we don't learn from our own mistakes. It's smart when we learn from our mistakes. However, it's wise when we learn from other people's mistakes.' As I said, this handbook is a collection. In the process of browsing through this, should you become educated, motivated or even wise along the way, so much the better.

"My goal is to be a trusted advisor and an advocate for my clients"

Karl N Kindschi, LUTCF

Contents

A True Story

When push comes to shove, I'm a life insurance agent. My first recollection of life insurance was the time I was old enough to take responsibility of my own policy. Taking responsibility meant the dubious honor of paying the premiums. I was eighteen. Years before that, my parents took out a policy on me and it was now time for me to take over.

Mom looked me right in the eye and said 'You <u>will</u> keep this policy up and you <u>will</u> pay the premiums on time! If you have trouble keeping the premiums up, let me know and we'll work something out, but <u>you will</u> pay these premiums!" We never had to 'work anything out' because I always paid the premium. I was afraid not to.

In 1984 I entered the life insurance business because of the sales opportunity it afforded me. I've always enjoyed meeting people, discovering their needs and providing a comfortable sales environment. I was entering the insurance industry at age 35 and my real education was about to begin. Being in the life insurance business was an exercise in discipline. The discipline of time management, human relations, continuing education and good, sound business decisions was very good for me. I enjoyed it then and I still do.

It wasn't until I helped a beneficiary settle a life insurance claim on a policy that I actually sold, that the 'life insurance business got in me'. This experience really defined to me, for all intents and purposes, what it actually meant to be a families' life insurance agent. I introduced myself to someone I didn't know, I worked with them to discover their needs and the budget they had to work with and I developed a couple of solutions. One of those solutions was put into place and two life insurance policies were issued. Neither of us thought that the family would be so dependent on one of those policies so soon.

Within seven months of those policies being delivered, I read about the accident in the newspaper. I was stunned. After preparing myself and reviewing procedures, I contacted the family.

I found out one very important underlying principle. It's one thing to respectfully attend a funeral, bring flowers and to mourn with the family. It's what most friends and relatives do. It's quite another thing to attend the funeral, bring flowers, to mourn and then to come back a couple days later with a check for $442,000. Everybody else brought flowers. I brought a check.

We cannot take away the emotional pain and suffering that a family must endure when a loved one is lost. We cannot wipe away the tears. We cannot fill the emptiness. But I could make sure that those kids didn't have to suffer even more emotional trauma by having to move from the only home they ever knew into an apartment. I could make sure that their education was already paid for. I could make sure that the families' income needs were taken care of. This is what life insurance is all about.

Life insurance has become so complex that agents need to be licensed in securities in order to provide competitive products. In doing so, conversations have a natural drift towards investments, rates of return and 'performance' rather than what the life contract is mainly purchased for; protecting someone you love. Having 'love' in your life sometimes means having the financial responsibility to take care of someone, whether you're still here or not.

This is also what being a life insurance agent is all about. These days, some life insurance agents are somewhat embarrassed about being called life insurance agents. Being a 'Financial Planner' or a 'Financial Consultant' is more to their taste. It's disconcerting to some when they are referred to as a life insurance agent. Some call themselves everything but life insurance agents. I am a life insurance agent and I provide protection for my clients.

> "I cannot think of any need in childhood as strong as the need for a father's protection. "
>
> Sigmund Freud (1856-1939)

Ten Years Ago

"Things do not change; we change. "

Henry David Thoreau (1817-1862),
U.S. philosopher, author, naturalist

Let's go through a 'time warp' together, you and me. Let's go back ten years ago and check things out. What were you actually doing ten years ago? If you have a picture of yourself taken 10 years ago, I would suppose that your looks have changed some. Perhaps your clothes look a little different. Perhaps your hairstyle has changed too. When I look back at my pictures of ten years ago, I'm a little embarrassed as to how I looked.

Did you have the same job as you do now, or is it different? What about your family life? What was your family doing ten years ago? I suppose you were like everybody else and had some problems or challenges way back there ten years ago. What opportunities where there for you? What were your dreams and goals?

If you had to list the things in your life that have changed in the last ten years, you might be surprised to realize that it's a long list! Another way of looking at it might be 'what things in my life have stayed the same during the last ten years'?

How was your health, your weight, and your stamina? I'll bet you a nickel that you've had some major changes in your life during the last ten years and your life today is different. Change occurs in all of our lives.

Now let's go through a different 'time warp'. This time let's leap ahead ten years from now into the future. That's right...ten years from now! Let's see...what do you suppose you'll be doing ten years from now? Would you expect that there are going to be a few changes in your life? Do you think you'll have the same job or the same career? What do you think the price of gasoline will be, or your mortgage payment, or your net worth?

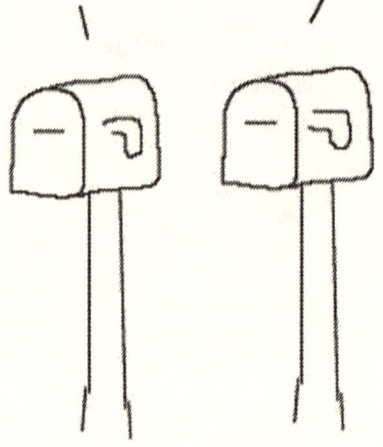

Do you suppose that you'll even be alive ten years from now? And how about your immediate family? Would you suppose that the makeup of your family would change? There may be some additions to your immediate or extended family, such as births or marriages or adoptions in ten years. There may very well be some family members or close friends who may not be here in another ten years. That's life isn't it? Life just doesn't stay the same, at least for very long.

"Change your opinions, keep to your principles; change your leaves, keep intact your roots"

Victor Hugo (1802-1885), French poet

Change is all around us. You can't go from one day to the next without experiencing some kind of change. These various changes are so unique because they all seem to effect us so differently. None of them are exactly the same. Some of these changes can be immense, 'life changing' events that startle us and change us forever. We never forget them nor do we forget the time they occurred.

But most of the changes that occur to us are little, sneaky changes. They sneak up on us when we are busy, or are distracted by other things. We weren't even paying attention. A lot of times we don't even realize that these little changes have even happened to us. We were just busy with other things at the time. We were busy with life. Who has time to observe?

Change can alter our opinions too. Our opinions and values are what make us who we are. Everyone has opinions. We even know how our best friends will react to circumstances before they happen. Because we know their opinions and values so well, we just know how they'll react to things.

There can be a problem with opinions though. We have a strong tendency to maintain our 'opinions' for maybe a little too long. We can more easily recognize this in other people. We recognize those opinions that have become slightly outdated. Sometimes people have a real collection of these outdated opinions. Ironically, most of these people usually are very verbal. Do you remember Archie Bunker? He had one of the largest collections of outdated opinions in the history of sitcom television.

Seriously, we tend to hang on to our opinions because they are so personal to us. We formed the opinions that we have. They are ours and they belong to us! They were formed based on what our lives and our values were at the time those opinions were made. There certainly isn't anything wrong with that.

Here's something scary, every once in a while, we realize that some of our opinions are exactly the same as our parents. Now, how could that happen? Surely I wouldn't be so easily influenced by my own parents. Would I?

Some of us are more opinionated than others. That's OK. Some of us tend to go with the flow and some of us tend to be more vocal and forceful. However, as our experience grows, we all hopefully mature and we not only notice that change occurs in our lives, but we embrace it. Only when we take stock in ourselves and look at where we are today, and where we were yesterday, we might find that our opinions and values and our goals have really changed a lot. Especially when you look backwards in a time frame of ten years or longer.

Here's the problem. We have been going merrily along our so-called 'normal lives' behaving as if nothing has ever changed over the years. Our spending and savings habits are the same as when we had our first job! Although our goals have changed and our income has changed, we haven't taken the time to adjust our compass so that we can even achieve our new goals. There is a certain amount of procrastination that sometimes occurs too. By in large, procrastination sneaks up on us and makes us complacent. When we least expect it, procrastination will hurt us. It hurts us in broken relationships, opportunities lost or, more often than not, procrastination hurts us in the wallet.

So, I suppose the key is to recognize and embrace change in our lives and be flexible enough to adjust our attitudes and our habits for our own good. Keep an open mind.

Challenge Questions

What was the most dramatic change in my life during the last 10 years?

_____

_____

What was the next most dramatic change?

_____

_____

How have those changes affected my opinions?

_____

_____

How have those changes affected my finances?

_____

_____

The Three Bears

"It is not okay when you get sick, or when you die, to leave financial chaos for those around you to bear the grief of your terrible illness or death: imagine for a minute, their pain. Please don't force them to deal as well with all the matters you could have taken care of while you were healthy or alive."

Suze Orman
The 9 steps To Financial Freedom
Crown Publishers, Inc.

Once upon a time there were three Bears, Momma Bear, Papa Bear and Baby Bear. Momma Bear worked outside the home as a registered nurse at the hospital emergency room. Since she has seniority, Momma Bear works the day shift after Baby Bear goes to elementary school. Actually 'Baby Bear' is a misnomer since 'Baby Bear' is seven and a half and is in the second grade. But everybody still calls Baby Bear 'Baby Bear' regardless of her age and she doesn't seem to mind. Yes, Baby Bear is a girl Bear.

Papa Bear is an engineer at a plastics firm on the outskirts of town. Papa Bear earned his bachelors degree in mechanical engineering fifteen years ago and has worked at the same manufacturing plant since graduation. Papa Bear earns a nice income, is satisfied with his work and is a member of a local service club. Other than fishing, his main pastime outside of work is a beekeeper and on the weekends mostly, he tends to his six beehives.

Momma and Papa Bear have been married for ten years and are thinking about getting a will drafted as soon as they have some spare time. They believe that in another ten years or so they should start thinking seriously about retirement planning. Since Papa Bear wants to work for another 20 years or so there is plenty of time to talk about 'retirement'. Retirement, after all, is for old Bears.

One day during a cold spell in the middle of winter, Papa Bear didn't come home. Driving home on an icy road, Papa Bear lost control of his car. It spun around a couple times, slid off into a steep embankment and landed on it's roof. Papa Bear landed quite awkwardly and never regained consciousness. He was pronounced dead at the scene.

A week after Papa Bear's funeral, Mamma Bear met with her insurance agent. She hadn't met this agent before. Papa Bear had a life insurance policy that he had as a teen-ager Bear. Mama Bear was the beneficiary, but the amount that she was going to receive was just enough to buy groceries and her other expenses for about eight months or so.

Papa Bear didn't believe in insurance really. His contributions into his company's 401K along with some matching funds from the company was 'more than enough' for the family. Mama Bear was surprised to learn that by using that 401K money for living expenses before she was of retirement age, that would trigger an IRS 'Pre-distribution penalty' of 10%, would be considered 'earned income', be subject to withholding and other income taxes and would thereby spend her entire retirement account before she would even approach retirement age.

Not only were her housing in jeopardy, but also Baby Bear's college fund, which they were going to get started soon, was now likely never to exist at all.

Mama Bear was becoming an unhappy camper. Particularly because a camper was about all that it seemed she could afford to live in right now. She was more emotional, stressed out, and it seemed every aspect of her life was in total, uncontrolled disarray. She was in chaos and really needed help.

Panda Bear, one of her co-workers at the hospital, shared some thoughts with Mama Bear during one of their breaks. Panda Bear shared with her how they were handling insurance and finances in their home.

Panda Bear said, 'Every year my husband and I sit down with our advisor and go over things. Every year, different things happen in our family situation that cause us to re-think our priorities.' Panda Bear continued, 'One year, my husband changed jobs and we needed to rollover his retirement plan. Another year when our child was born, we needed to update our life insurance beneficiaries and at the same time, we re-evaluated our life insurance amounts. It was a little surprising when we added up the amounts we were going to actually need in case something would happen to either one of us.'

"But every jet of chaos which threatens to exterminate us, is convertible by intellect into wholesome force. "

Ralph Waldo Emerson (1803–1882)

'Another time we evaluated things like our wills and we even got a trust started. Our advisor helped arrange an appointment with an attorney. The attorney even recommended drafting a 'Durable Power of Attorney' and a 'Living Will'.

'We've known our advisor for a number of years now, we've done some business with him over the years, but we mostly appreciate the organized approach he has toward the big picture…our big picture. You should see him!'

Mama Bear did. But she wished she'd done it sooner. Change occurred in the Bear family also, but they ignored it and chaos ensued.

Challenge Questions

How long has it been since I've reviewed my insurance plans?

_____

_____

What things have changed in my life since I've updated my insurance plans?

_____

_____

How confident am I that my insurance plans are at the proper level for me?

_____

_____

I could use a little help!

_____

_____

Different Eyes

We need to have a discussion about your eyes. Your eyes are extremely important to you. So, tell me, what do you see? In an art gallery, a room full of people can look at the same piece of artwork and all see different things.

Our vision of the world in which we live is a matter of our perspective. The perspective you have after reading a classical novel, for example, is one thing. But when you read that same novel fifteen years later, you may have a different perspective on it. The eyes that read that novel are different eyes that read it fifteen years ago. One discovers another level of understanding. Perhaps there is a sub-plot that you hadn't noticed before. The characters portrayed have a different, unspoken intent that wasn't there the first time. The story has a fresh twist to it.

We hadn't noticed it before. Our eyes have changed. They have become more experienced eyes with a slightly different perspective.

That book really hadn't changed at all. It was published years ago. It hadn't changed, we changed. We matured a little, that's all. If we would read it again fifteen years from now, we might peel away still another layer of understanding. I suppose that is what essentially defines a 'classic' in that it offers as many levels of understanding as there are readers having various levels of perception. I believe music and art is exactly the same. Actually, anything of quality seems to have this trait.

"The world itself looks cleaner and so much more beautiful. Maybe we can make it that way—the way God intended it to be—by giving everyone, eventually, that new perspective from out in space."

Roger B Chaffee, US astronaut
In his last public interview before he died with astronauts Virgil I Grissom and Edward H White II in a fire aboard Apollo 1 during a simulated launch, *This Week* 23 Apr 67

You could
Look at it
this way.

Or, you
could look
at it this way!

Applying this principle to finances and insurance is appropriate. First of all, let's be honest with each other. When you sit down with an insurance agent, this is about the very last thing that you really want to do. I know. Some of you have actually told this to me. Somehow you are being forced to do it. You don't want to do it and you want to get it over with just as fast as you can–and have your wallet still intact. It's painful. It's also painful when an agent has to come back to the survivors and explain the pitifully small amount they have coming.

I remember meeting with a widow to file the life insurance death benefit claim papers on her husband's policy. This was my very first death claim as an agent. That policy was over forty years old. That 'writing agent' had long since retired. As she and I met at her kitchen table, I was completing the necessary paperwork. Right smack in the middle of the table, next to the salt and pepper shakers and napkin holder, was a stack of various bills that needed to be paid. I couldn't help but notice them. I was mentally adding them up in my head. I subtracted them from the life insurance proceeds and quickly determined that this nice little lady's financial future was not good. I thought to myself that this life insurance policy would be the last act of love of the deceased. Some act of love. This 'act of love' put her into a financial mess for the remainder of her life.

Loving memories can be cut short after the realism of a non-loving, financially selfish act of negligence takes its place. I've seen it and it's not pretty…for anybody involved.

All I can say is, 'Poor planning will always result in poor results'.

'Once you have been confronted with a life-and-death situation, trivia no longer matters. Your perspective grows and you live at a deeper level. There's no time for pettiness.'

Margaretta ("Happy") Rockefeller
On recovery from cancer, *Family Weekly* 9 May 76

You also need to know that others' eyes change too. You are not the only one who changes. The eyes of your advisor changes also. Don't think that your advisor can't learn a thing or two as time goes on.

In the 1990's, the rules changed which regulated licensed agents in Wisconsin. That law mandated a certain number of 'pre-licensing' hours of study for a new insurance agent to become licensed. That was a good thing.

Another good thing was the continuing education requirement necessary for a licensed intermediary, an agent, to continue to keep his or her license. This was a great thing for the buying public because it helped make sure that their advisor, or agent would be more likely to be kept up-to-date on insurance and other financial issues.

Still another thought about learning is this. I've expressed the thought on many occasions that some of the most fabulous ideas that I've been able to collect came directly from my clients during our interviews together. I simply pass them on. We can learn a lot from each other. Our perspective can always improve.

"Because fully functioning people are always exploring new areas and wandering around in the unknown, they are constantly bumping into new ideas and attitudes."

Dr. Wayne Dyer
The Sky's the Limit
Simon and Schuster, page 278

Challenge Questions

What new perspective do I have now that I didn't when I was younger?

_____

_____

How has that changed my decision-making?

_____

_____

What book or movie have I enjoyed just as much or more the second time?

_____

_____

Developing Understanding

> "There are three principal means of acquiring knowledge available to us: observation of nature, reflection, and experimentation. Observation collects facts; reflection combines them; experimentation verifies the result of that combination. Our observation of nature must be diligent, our reflection profound, and our experiments exact. We rarely see these three means combined; and for this reason, creative geniuses are not common."
>
> Denis Diderot (1713–1784), French philosopher

The very first time a new concept is posed to you that you have never considered, or even heard of, do you believe that your first impulse or your first response will reflect your true feelings? After reflection and some reconsideration, you might find yourself having a different point of view than what you originally expressed.

The value of working with a trusted advisor can be beneficial at the level of helping you take some time and think of what has indeed changed over the years.

A trusted advisor can ask you identical questions that were asked of you ten years ago and guess what? Your answers are completely different now! Now, how could that be? What that could mean is that you could be a totally different person now! Your life situation is on a totally different track! You may have different values or a different perspective. This shouldn't come as a surprise, but it seems it always does.

After a death in the family, a person can re-evaluate their need for life insurance, and all of a sudden have a different understanding as to the necessity of a large amount of ready cash.

I have another question for you. Have you ever found yourself discussing a personal matter or a problem with someone you trust? Someone you would trust with your life. Perhaps you needed to make a difficult decision and you were having quite a time with it. In the course of that discussion, while you were verbalizing, the answer gradually emerged. It became more and more clear as you verbalized it. Sometimes your close friend may not have even said a word. You might have solved it all by yourself. You just needed to say it out loud and it became clear!

This is also what a trusted financial advisor can, and should, be able to do for you. The advisor simply has the structure for the conversation. All you have to do is to personalize the structure to fit you. Your goals are your goals. Your opinions are your opinions. Your dreams are your dreams!

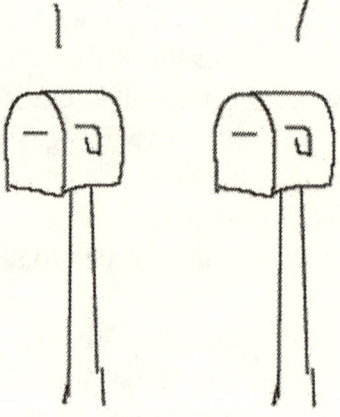

Another huge advantage your trusted financial advisor can bring to the table are those experienced eyes. Experience is something one cannot buy. Remember the phrase, 'If I'd only known then what I know now! Boy, I'd do things differently!' Your advisor should be able to keep you from going down a very bad road. That road should be going in the direction of your goals and dreams. This has to be your road, not anyone else's. Perhaps…a road less traveled.

"I shall be telling this with a sigh
Somewhere ages and ages hence:
Two roads diverged in a wood, and I –
I took the one less traveled by,
And that has made all the difference."

Robert Frost
The Road Not Taken
Holt, Rinehart and Winston

Offense & Defense

All sporting events have elements of offense and defense. Basketball, baseball, soccer, volleyball and every other sport I can think of have an offense and a defense. Some sports, such as football, have separate players that play positions either designated as a defense or offensive position. Those players only have one specialty, as a defensive or offensive player.

As we play different card games, we can play aggressively or defensively. In euchre, there is a term called 'guarding the gate' in which teammates play a defensive posture. There are countless examples.

Even driving a car can be a defensive or an offensive experience. During the course of driving a vehicle, there are virtually an unlimited number of decisions to be made. How fast should I drive? How close to the car ahead of me should I be? How soon should I turn on the directionals? When should I pass? When do I pull out into traffic? Where should I position the vehicle in relation to the lane? How should I be merging into traffic? The list goes on and on.

We've all experienced uncomfortable times when a driver in the car in which we're a passenger drives a little too fast, or a little too close, or a little too irresponsible for our taste. Addressing the issue can be a direct slam on that driver's personal integrity. The driving experience, after all, is an accumulation of the results of all that driver's decisions. It's a personal thing.

How much of our everyday lives are done subconsciously? I believe that most everything we buy can be attributed to either an offensive purchase or a defensive purchase. Chain restaurants across the country sell the same menu items. To the weary traveler, pulling in to a familiar restaurant means that we will not be disappointed in our meal choice. We've had it before in our hometown. That is a defensive purchase. We bought it because we knew we probably wouldn't be disappointed. It has been said that we make most of our decisions subconsciously, on a defensive basis.

At other times we make purchases that we are pretty sure it will make us feel great! A brand new suit or a sensational new outfit makes us feel good about ourselves. It makes us feel successful because we look successful. We walk a little taller, we feel a little trimmer, and we gain a certain confidence because we feel great. We are looking good!

That purchase is an 'offensive purchase' because by buying that brand new suit, with the altering that makes it fit us precisely and individually, we become someone better. We develop a better quality of ourselves; our self-image grows, we become a little bit more what we know we can be. We find ourselves being someone to look up to. Now that offense is going somewhere!

Financial and Insurance products could be generally categorized the same way. They could be envisioned as either offensive or defensive in nature.

Starting <u>Offensive</u> Line Up	Starting <u>Defensive</u> line Up
Annuities	Life Insurance
Mutual funds	Health Insurance
Stocks	Long Term Care
Bonds	Disability Insurance
IRA's	Homeowners Insurance
401 K's	Automobile Insurance
Real Estate	Liability (Umbrella) Policies

As an example, consider a homeowners insurance policy. That would be a defensive product. It is defensive in the fact that in case of a fire, that insurance policy would replace the damage that was done and restore the owner to the same position he/she was in prior to the fire. In case of a loss, you are restored. That is defense.

A mutual fund, on the other hand, would be an example of an offensive purchase. The reason to make that purchase would be to put yourself into a better position in the future. Your objective would be to grow and to move forward.

Great Teams have both
excellent OFFENSIVE and
DEFENSIVE units!

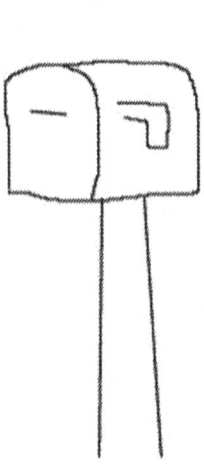

Some financial products can be a little of both. They can be defensive and offensive at the same time (No pun intended). As an example, a Variable Life Insurance Policy has insurance protection for an individual with underlying 'sub-accounts'. The sub-accounts are similar to mutual funds in a way. They both are considered investments capable of being either very conservative or aggressive. There is a wide choice of sub-accounts with the policy because the insurance companies want them to appeal to a wide variety of clients. Those investment 'sub-accounts' are designed to grow faster than ordinary life insurance choices. So you have both protection and growth in the same product.

"True balance demands that we determine what accomplishments give us honest satisfaction as well as what failures cause us intolerable grief."

Melinda M. Marshall (20th century), U.S. writer and editor

Concentrate on only ONE TOPIC at a time.

"To be what you are and to become what you are capable of becoming is the secret of a happy life."

Og Mandino, The Greatest Success In The World,
Bantam Books,

You didn't become the successful person you are overnight. So don't expect to try to solve all of the things you want to change overnight either. To use the vernacular, 'Don't try to choke a horse', or don't try to do everything at once.

The world we live in is a complicated place. Information flies at us every day at a pace that is numbing. Product and service advertisements hit us more times in the course of one day than what hit our grandparents during their entire lifetime.

There has never been a period in the history of mankind that we've had a greater number of opportunities for ourselves. Products, business opportunities, toys, new prescription drugs and worldwide topics and issues abound. We have more career opportunities, more ways of expressing ourselves, more choices of the foods we eat, more entertainment choices and more financial plans to choose from. There are more ways to expand our individual wealth than ever before.

There are also more ways to go into debt and financial trouble than ever before.

We spend far less time in our personal financial planning than we should. Maybe it's because we have become engulfed in all the mind-numbing choices we have in the more exciting areas of our lives. Most of us don't like to spend time in our financial planning.

So, then it must be a matter of discipline. It's a matter of discipline in the fact that we must force ourselves to become educated in an ever-expanding number of these new 'products and opportunities' which we are faced with everyday.

The system I've developed over the years was built to be sensitive to the never-ending array of personal, family and business situations that come up and have to be dealt with. There are too many topics, too many decisions and never enough finances available to deal with it all satisfactorily in one fell swoop.

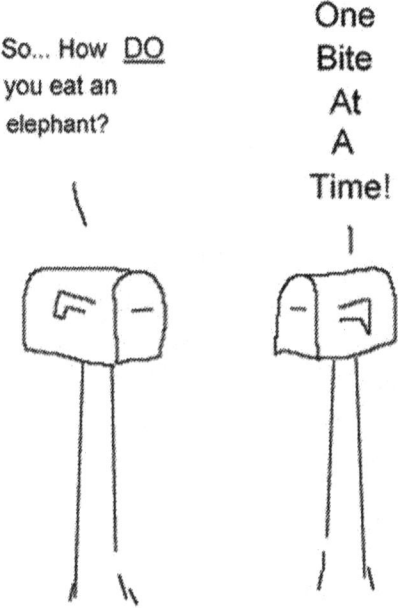

I've met and done some business with millionaires. Millionaires are not unlike many other people in the fact that they simply do not have, nor do they want a bunch of extra money lying around, 'just in case'. Their assets are out working somewhere. Some of it is in real estate, some of it is earning interest, and some of it is earning dividends. Most of it is off making even more money somewhere else. Money is like a lot of other entities. Some of it works harder than others. Some of it is in 'defensive' products and some of it is on the 'offense'.

However, in virtually every case, whether a person is a millionaire or not, discussions and decisions are made one at a time. Ample time is needed to gather pertinent information, discuss options and opportunities with qualified, trusted advisors, and then to act accordingly. An offensive team and a defensive team cannot both be on the football field at the same time. Take it one at a time and never try to do everything at once.

"I focus on my role as plant manager. I can't help the fact that I'm a black, woman plant manager. I have to make the…decisions…my job requires."

Deborah S. Kent (1953–)

Challenge Questions

What experience have I had that caused me to focus intently on something for an extended period of time?

_____

_____

What was the result of that extended focus?

_____

_____

How often do I focus intently on goals that matter to me?

_____

_____

If I purposefully focus on a major goal of mine, on a regular basis, what do I think the result would be?

_____

_____

Review Dates

"…Both success and failure are largely the results of habit!"

Napoleon Hill
Think and Grow Rich
Fawcett Crest Books, page 86

The easiest decision for you to make is the 'Review Date' decision. This is the decision of 'which month' do you prefer to have your own personal reviews conducted. This is the month that each year you will plan on carving out time to review things, learn about things, set priorities and to do some implementing.

Only you can know what's best for you. Some parts of the year will be an automatic 'out'. Some parts of each year should lend itself to be more favorable to schedule some thoughtful time for you.

On those 'defensive' products such as insurance, there are birth dates to consider. Some policies really do care what age you are. So if you were to initiate such a plan, it would benefit you to do it prior to a birthday. There is no sense in throwing money away.

Should you have trouble finding a month's time frame to be able to set aside for yourself and you just can't commit to setting aside a particular month in which you'll need a couple two hour segments, you'll need to take a crash course in time management.

There are also some very good 'self-esteem' courses available. Actually, there are some among us who have this overwhelming need to take much better care of others than of themselves. Let's get real. If you cannot take care of yourself, you will be in absolutely no shape to take care of anyone else. Shape up.

When you choose the most appropriate month for your review to occur, the 'Annual Review Process' kicks in and keeps the process on track for reviews. Reminders are automatically sent to clients the month prior to your review month.

Not only does the system make sense, you will appreciate it as years go by and you will actually look forward to it. You feel good just knowing that you 'have a plan' even if it's just a plan to 'work on your plan'!

The Importance of Annual Reviews

"The more genuine the involvement, the more sincere and sustained the participation in analyzing and solving problems, the greater the release of everyone's creativity, and of their commitment to what they create."

Stephen R Covey, The 7 Habits of Highly Effective People, Simon & Schuster

I have concentrated my work on the three most important areas of my client's financial life. Those three areas are:

1. 'Savings & Retirement Management'
2. 'Personal Risk Management'
3. 'Business & Estate Protection'.

The process, which I have gradually developed and used over the years, I call the 'Annual Client Review System'. It is a relaxed, routine and systematic process which clients really feel comfortable with. The planning process which clients experience as they progress through the system becomes natural, more complete and precise to each client as time goes on.

Each client has a unique and individual program, which is developed as time goes on. In this distinct system, time works for you versus working against you.

Clients start with the most critical topic that happens to be important to them at that particular time. We progress from there. As time goes on, their plan develops and is reviewed on a regular basis. The intent is that we avoid future crisis by monitoring progress against the goals each client has set for himself or herself.

As Napoleon Hill surmised in his book 'Think and Grow Rich', both success and failure are largely the results of habit. It is very important for you to avoid the bad habits, especially the bad financial bad habits. Bad financial habits allow time to work against you each and every day. There is too much stress in our lives the way it is without asking for it each and every day. Life is far too short.

You and I, together, develop good financial habits. Annual reviews provide you the opportunity to have time work for you. We review your program annually. In some instances we may get together more often, but that typically happens only in the first year or so because there are a number of topics that simply must be covered. That's OK, but normally we'll meet annually. That is my commitment to you.

Challenge Questions

What month would typically be good for me, each year, to take some extra time for myself and set a few exciting personal goals?

_____

_____

Why would that particular month be good for me?

_____

_____

What month or months do I want to avoid at all costs?

_____

_____

Presenting...
The Annual
Client Review
System !

Annual Client Review System

Have you ever bought an insurance product or an investment product and never saw that agent or representative again? When you've bought a policy or a contract and had it delivered to you and everything was 'just fine', did that agent or representative thank you, walk out the door and not schedule your next review? Has the 'next visit' been pretty much 'open-ended'? Have you noticed that literally 'years' have gone by without much contact or any contact at all?

If this has ever happened to you, you will fall in love with this system...the 'Annual Client Review System'. This is how it works.

Since every client is unique and is surrounded by unique circumstances. It is impossible to fit everyone into the same program, at the same time with the same products. It just doesn't work and it's not fair to anybody.

This is the process. When I begin working with a prospective client, you for example, there normally is a 'hot topic' that you need to deal with, or there is something you are particularly interested in.

Two things need to happen at this point. One–I need to know about you and why that particular 'hot topic' is hot with you. Two–you need to know who I am, what my qualifications are, what I commit to do for you as my client, and how I go about my work.

Let's begin with the Annual Client Review System. Think of the work we'll be doing together as divided into three equal parts.

This graph represents all of the general categories of topics we'll eventually discuss over the next three (3) years. The three categories are 'Personal Risk Management', 'Savings & Retirement Management' and 'Business & Estate Protection'.

Annual Client Review System

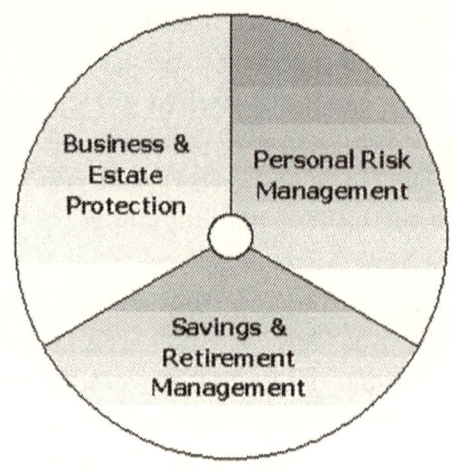

We can't deal with every issue at the same time, so you will need to choose just one area to begin with. Generally this won't be a problem because there is typically one 'hot topic' we need to deal with. Eventually we'll be going over all three areas.

The First Year

Let's assume that the reason we got together in the first place was that you are shopping around for health insurance. In that case, we'll be talking about the 'Personal Risk Management' category.

Personal Risk Management

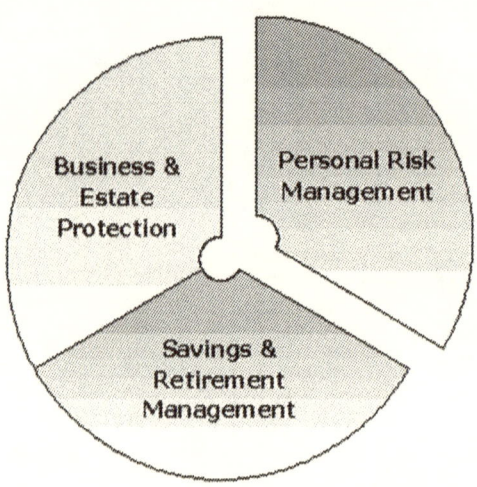

This category talks about protecting the people you love by having adequate health insurance as well as replacing your income, paying for various expenses, etc.

'Programming' is a term used for gathering all pertinent facts and data regarding a particular subject, then analyzing that situation in order to present one or more solutions to the problem, if any problem exists. Programming enables clients to re-assess their personal insurance needs and really should be done on a regular basis.

The types of products that are in this area of conversation include:

Health Insurance	Life Insurance
Medicare Supplements	Homeowners Insurance
Long Term Care Policies	Automobile Insurance
Nursing Home Policies	Excess Liability Insurance
Income Protection	Etc.

More on 'Risk Management'

> "Life insurance, even when it is not purchased for its investment characteristics, is still a part of planning for financial security. In its simplest application, if anyone depends upon your income, then you need life insurance."
>
> Ellie Williams
> Investor's Desk Reference
> McGraw-Hill

How do you handle risk? As far as I can tell, there are only four ways to deal with risk. This would include any risk you can think of. You can avoid it, reduce it, assume it or transfer it.

Most of us drive cars so let's use that as an illustration. When dealing with the risk of having a car accident, we could avoid it altogether. By simply never owning or driving a car, it would be impossible to crash one. Although being a passenger in a crashed car would still be a problem unless we avoid that possibility also by not ever riding in a car.

A little less dramatic, we could reduce the risk. By driving at a slower and a safer speed, by using alternate, less traveled routes and perhaps keeping our car in good repair, we could reduce the risks associated with driving.

Another but quite risky option would be to <u>assume the risk</u>. By driving without insurance an operator assumes the financial responsibility to people who may be injured or to families of persons who died as a result of accidents you caused. Most people simply do not have hundreds of thousands or millions of dollars readily available to pay out to claimants of those who you, albeit accidentally, injure or kill. The thought of losing all of your future paychecks for the remainder of your life and sending it to accident victims is not a cherished thought.

The alternative to this would be to <u>transfer the risk</u>. That is, purchase adequate auto insurance from a reputable insurance carrier, that would be sufficient in paying claims, after a deductible amount is first paid by you, to the injured party. You've just transferred that risk to someone else. In this case, that someone else is an insurance company. For that privilege, the insurance company charges you a 'premium'. This frees up that entire inordinate amount of cash you'd otherwise have to have laying around 'just in case'.

Nice alternative, but you absolutely must review your insurance coverages on a regular basis. To have inadequate amounts of coverage destroys the very reason why you have it in the first place.

Sometimes, as a practical matter, it is prudent to do two things simultaneously. For example, transfer the risk by purchasing a policy and to reduce the risk by getting in the habit of slowing down.

Another example might be the risk of house fire. You could <u>avoid it</u> by not living in a house. You could live in a tent.

If you prefer to live in a house, you could <u>reduce the risk</u> of house fire by buying smoke detectors, fire extinguishers, conducting fire drills, installing a sprinkler system and even having the fire department conduct an inspection. These are all good things.

<u>Assuming this risk</u> would mean to cancel your Homeowners Insurance policy. You'd also need to pay off the mortgage at the same time because your banker or lending institution will call and demand the mortgage to be paid. If a fire burned the house down, you'd need to pay for another house all over again though.

Or you could <u>transfer the risk</u> of that house fire. When you purchase adequate amounts of homeowners insurance, the risk is now borne by the insurance company in exchange for a premium. The premium will have a lot to do with the size and type of home you have, how close you are to a fire department, etc.

The typical Property & Casualty policies include:

Home

Auto

Umbrella (Excess Liability)

Regarding Life Insurance, there are a lot of reasons why people need life insurance. Here are some of them:

- To 'Fund' A Business Transfer
- To Pay Last Expenses
- To Pay Off The Home Mortgage
- To Pay Death Taxes & Estate Settlement Costs
- To Provide A Charitable Gift
- To Provide Benefits to a 'Key Employee'
- To Pay Off Loans
- To Equalize Inheritances
- To Replace Gifts To A 'Charitable Remainder Trust'
- To Replace The Loss of A 'Group Term' Policy
- To Create An Estate
- To Provide Income For A Spouse

Occasionally, young families will want to provide money for their children's college expenses even if they should not survive until their children reach college age. Life insurance is the most prudent solution for that purpose. It provides the necessary cash even if the parent does not live long enough to even earn the money to help pay for those future college costs.

Of all the insurance policies that you will ever own in your lifetime, the only one that will pay for sure is the policy on your life. It is the only policy that is not insuring against a **possibility**. Your life insurance policy insures against a **guaranteed certainty**. Everybody is going to die some day, we just don't know WHEN! The trick is to financially insure your family from you dieing too early! Doesn't seem fair does it!

It must be something in our human nature, because so many people don't think twice about purchasing insurance to cover a fairly remote possibility of their home burning down, but can't quite bring themselves to purchase insurance to cover an absolute certainty, losing their life.

Actually, the only groups of <u>people who will not require life insurance</u> are those who will not leave someone or something behind who they care about, and those who will not leave any bills to pay or financial commitments to fulfill.

Also, life insurance is also the only insurance contract that provides a benefit, which is paid to someone else other than the insured. The beneficiary receives the benefits of a life contract. Other insurance products such as auto, homeowners, disability income and business insurance pay the policyholder, the owner, directly. Those policies provide a benefit payable to the insured.

There are important Health Insurance topics and products included in this category also. Some of those include:

Long Term Care	Major Medical
Disability Income	PPO
Medicare	Specialty Health Insurance
Medicare Supplement	Cancer Insurance Policies
Group Health Insurance	Dental Policies

The Second Year

The next area we discuss would be the 'Savings & Retirement Management' category. In this discussion, we talk specifically about how much you are currently saving for yourself, what accounts do you already have established, are you diversified properly, and are you on track to achieve your retirement goal?

Savings & Retirement Management

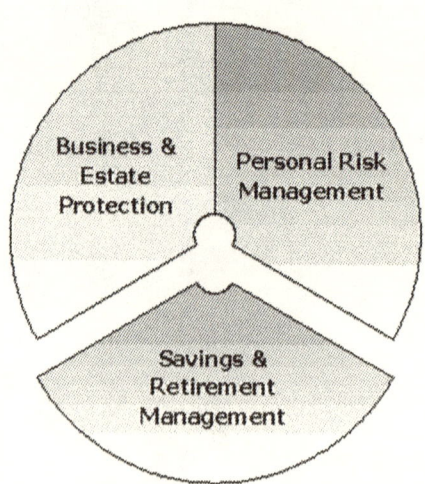

At any given moment, clients differ in their affluence, ability to manage money, interest in managing money, personal preferences, risk tolerance and investment goals. Together, we identify appropriate diversification of assets.

It's interesting to note that as time goes marching on, people tend to 'change their minds' on retirement issues. The challenge is to change it for the good! We have some real interesting discussions on this category. This is where your money is 'On The Offense".

Programming is a major tool in helping you in determining whether your plan is 'on track' to accomplish your goal, regardless whether that goal is 'College Funding', 'Retirement Planning', or simply saving money for a down payment on a home or business.

A short list of typical accounts and conversations on the 'Savings & Retirement Management' area includes:

401K/Pension Rollovers	Roth IRA's
Mutual Funds	Section 529 Plans for College
Qualified Annuities	CD's
Non-Qualified Annuities	Money Market Accounts
Settlement Options	Etc.
Traditional IRA's	

Challenge Questions

What percent (%) of my current income am I currently saving?

_____

_____

The following people are currently saving money for me so I'll have plenty of retirement income:

_____

_____

Who is responsible for my net worth?

_____

_____

My net worth increases some each year.   ❏   Yes   ❏   No

I could use some help in discovering my retirement options.

❏   Yes   ❏   No

More on Retirement Management

"Familiar basics for successful living could be easily applied to investing...
Commons Sense, Comfort Level, Diversification and Discipline."

        Esther M Berger, CFP
        First V.P. Paine Weber
        'Money Smart. Take The Fear Out of Financial Planning'
        Avon Books
        Simon & Schuster

The conversation regarding retirement issues is so interesting because everyone approaches it so differently. It is quite a personal, individual theme actually.

Some of the conversations we may have are included here:

- Understanding Social Security benefits
    - Social Security Offset

- Accumulation Phase

  What percent (%) of your income are you currently saving?

  Non-vested (Partially-vested) pensions

- Asset Allocation

  The importance of diversification regardless of risk tolerance

  Having emergency money available always

  The importance of reviews

  Personalized risk tolerance

  Asset Allocation is the blend of various types of stocks, bonds, cash and cash equivalents that make up your entire financial portfolio. It is unique to everyone. Your Asset Allocation may change because of:

  - A business sold
  - Inheritances
  - Pre-Retirement issues
  - Post-Retirement issues
  - Simply changing your mind or your opinion

- Distribution Phase

  Income Needs

  Pension Maximization

  Settlement Options

Another important benefit in regularly reviewing your plan is the ability to take advantage and maximize current laws and regulations. You wouldn't file your income tax return based on laws of 10 years ago would you? I wouldn't think so.

How many variables are there in retirement planning? There are as many variables as there are stars in the sky. What could change from year to year? Well, people may not think about it too often, so let's just list a couple.

1. How is inflation impacting my plan?
2. Rate of return on my money (Market Fluctuations)
3. Time left before I retire.
4. Who should be named as beneficiaries?
5. What investment choices should I make?
6. improved products are out there now?
7. Am I saving an adequate amount each month or each year?
8. Has my job or career change affected by benefits?
9. Has there been a change in the tax code or other law changes, which will affect my plan?
10. Is the lump-sum amount I planned on needing for retirement still adequate?

Each of these variables has impact. The consequences of not adjusting to those variables can have a severe impact on your life and of those in your inner closest circle. Don't forget that your spouse or your most immediate family will experience the result of your planning or lack thereof. So we want to make sure we get it right. Let me say that again. We want to make sure we get it right.

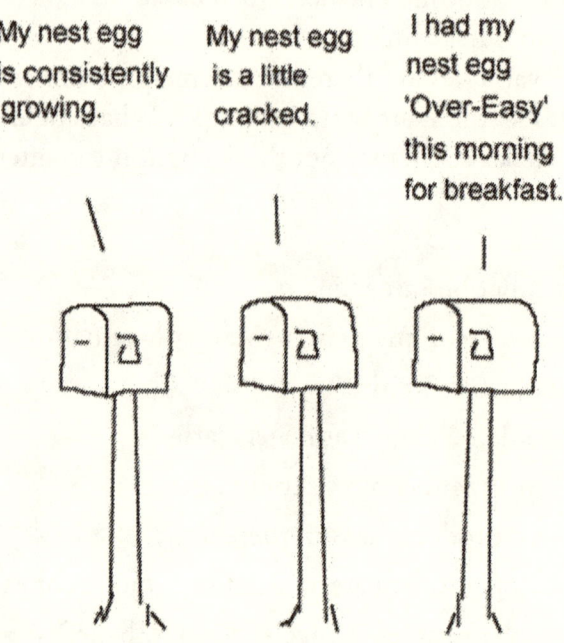

"Go/Go...Slow/Go...No/Go"

At retirement, the issues change. You now have a nest egg. A nest egg that is different from anyone else's. Your concerns are now different than anytime prior to this. There are many nest egg management concepts. Here is just one of them.

The Retirement Philosophy **"Go/Go...Slow/Go...No/Go"**. This philosophy divides your nest egg in three (3) totally separate investment groups. Each group is invested in ten (10) year time frames. The theory goes like this.

1. Go/Go–When you first retire, you are 'go, go', going all the time. You hardly stop! You are busier than when you where working! You ask yourself... 'How did I ever have time to work?' You'll need income for this 10-year period.

2. Slow/Go–After you get the traveling pretty much out of your system, or perhaps your health dictates to you to slow down, this is a time where you travel around, but not so much. You'll need income for this 10-year period also.

3. No/Go–This is the time when typically a person's health dictates that you had better stay home, or that your home now is a nursing home. You may need a lot of income for this 10-year period, or a long term care policy to help pay for it.

Each group of retirement money is invested in accordance to when the money will be needed. It's easier to manage when you can budget this way.

Retirement is similar to pre-retirement in some ways. The importance of staying invested is one of them. If being invested was important before retirement it is equally important during retirement.

The cost of living & inflation issues are still there. A person should be thinking of the future regardless of whether their income is coming from 'earned income' or 'un-earned income'. Understanding inflation risk is a basic building block of financial plans.

So a person should probably stay invested at all times to a certain extent. Having said that, it is just as important to ensure that your portfolio is suitable for you now that you are retired. This means that a normal and routine check on your asset allocation is in order.

The process really never stops. It shouldn't stop. There are always issues to consider and adjustments to make. In the last few years, companies have been able to produce some very good, simple worksheets that help you identify your 'comfort zone' or your 'suitability'.

There is a lot of attention to 'suitability' these days. That's good for you. That keeps your portfolio in balance and in working order for you.

Regarding retirement plans, there seems to be a large list of retirement options available. This is not an 'all-inclusive list' but it gives you a flavor of what choices are out there:

IRA's	Keogh
ROTH IRA's	SIMPLE IRA's
401K	SEP IRA's
Pension Money Purchase Plans	SARSEP IRA's
Pension Defined Benefit Plans	

These can all be funded by a variety of underlying investment products such as stocks, bonds, mutual funds, annuities, etc.

Managing inheritances is another topic that comes up from time to time. When it comes to inheritances, there are two different points of view, the receiving point of view and the giving point of view. I've worked with clients on both ends of this spectrum. At the same time, they are both exciting and concerning experiences.

When a person receives an inheritance, one doesn't want to make any mistakes that would be irreparable, so we take a thoughtful approach to inheritances.

One of the most exciting and rewarding experiences for a client is when they put an inheritance or a gifting program together. It is a special time in that by the act of 'gifting' it keeps a dream alive. That's exciting.

Challenge Questions

How long has it been since I've reviewed my investment plans?

_____

_____

What things have changed in my life since I've updated my investment plans?

_____

_____

How confident am I that my investment plans are at the proper level for me?

_____

_____

I could use a little help!

_____

_____

The Third Year

The final category is the 'Business & Estate Protection' area. This also varies widely, depending on each client's particular situation. If you own a business, we'll probably be asking questions like; 'How did you get into the business' and 'How are you planning on getting out of the business'? That's important if you ever plan on retiring.

Another example would be if you need any expert help in estate planning, if you would need a Will or any Trust documents drafted. This is as varied as the individual and since I am not an attorney or a CPA, I work with them, with your permission and on your behalf, to help put insurance or investment products together to fit your plan.

Business & Estate Protection

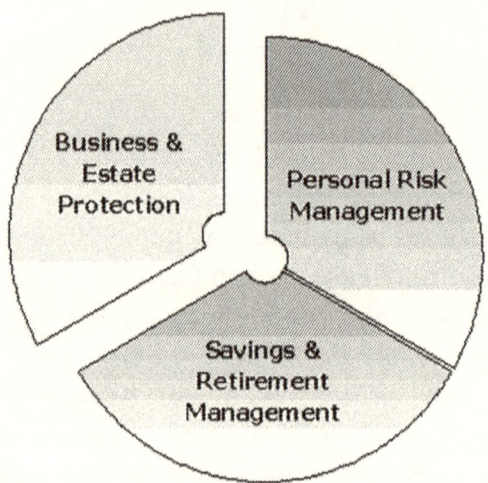

The basic objectives of business & estate planning are to provide for the orderly and efficient accumulation, conservation and distribution of assets, while avoiding conflict, shortening delays and reducing expenses.

Some of the products and conversations in this "Business & Estate Protection' area may include some of these:

'Funded' Buy-Sell Agreements	Wills
Last Survivor Life Insurance	Trusts
Annuities	Business Owners' P&C Policies
Gifting	Workman's Compensation

It must be noted here that I am not an attorney and I do not draft Wills nor do I set up Trust Documents, nor do I provide any opinion about those legal instruments. I leave that up to qualified legal counsel.

Not only would it be illegal for anyone other than qualified legal counsel to offer advice or opinion, you certainly want it all to work right. One time I heard an attorney compare a Last Will and Testament with a parachute. They are exactly the same things in the fact that they only need to work one time...and it better work!

My part in this equation is that I ask all of my clients if they have a current Will, Trust Documents and other legal papers in place. If not, then I strongly encourage them to visit an attorney as soon as possible. I feel that it is important for my clients to have pretty much everything in order.

It is surprising to me that young families often neglect to name a guardian for their children in the event of their deaths. The only place where parents can express their choice of guardians is in their Wills or Trust Documents. I guess people just don't think of those things.

Most property that you own probably has either a title or deed, or is a contract that will be assumed by another party at your death, or is a contract that is payable to a beneficiary, or is controlled by your Will or your Trust. All of these instruments that you own should be working together to accomplish your plans.

You are the quarterback of your own team. Your attorney, your accountant, your insurance agent, your financial advisor and any other professionals in your life, all need to be on the same page. I simply initiate the necessary discussions.

More on Business and Estate Protection

"The secret is: 'Mind your own business.' Financial struggle is often directly the result of people working all their life for someone else. Many people will have nothing at the end of their working days."

Robert T. Kiyosaki
Rich Dad, Poor Dad
TechPress, Inc

Some of the topics to be discussed will include:

- Minimizing the Federal Estate Taxes.

- Transferring Assets
    - Business Assets
    - Personal Assets
    - Gifting

- Organizing a Network of Experts
    - Attorney
    - Accountant
    - Insurance
    - Specialist
    - Financial Advisor
    - Stock Broker
    - Banker
    - Trust Officers
    - Other Professionals

The professionals you work with must have a good relationship with other professionals to maximize the results of your plan. Beware of him who disparages those in other professions. Today it is critical for professions to co-operate for the common good of the client.

Regarding Business Owners, these additional topics will be covered:

- Property & Casualty Insurance
    - Business (Commercial/Farm/Business Owners Policies)
    - Business Auto(s)
    - Umbrella (Excess Liability)

- Worker's Compensation

- Life Insurance
    - Business Succession Topics
    - Key Employee Benefits
    - Deferred Compensation

Is she or   Only her portfolio
isn't she?   manager knows
                for sure.

Challenge Questions

This is how I entered my career:

_____

_____

This is my plan for when I retire from my career:

_____

_____

My plan needs a little work.   ❑   Yes   ❑   No

I currently have a Will.   ❑   Yes   ❑   No

I currently have a 'Living Trust'.   ❑   Yes   ❑   No

I don't really know what legal work I should have done.
                                     ❑   Yes   ❑   No

The Fourth Year

Now we are at the beginning of the fourth year. What have we accomplished so far? Although this may have taken three years, you've gone through the cycle! The Annual Client Review System! It works! Your program is on the way to superior performance for you!

You'll also notice that we took 'one step at a time' and it really didn't hurt one bit! Here is the magic of the system...the next step will be to start over with the very first one. That's right, we start all over.

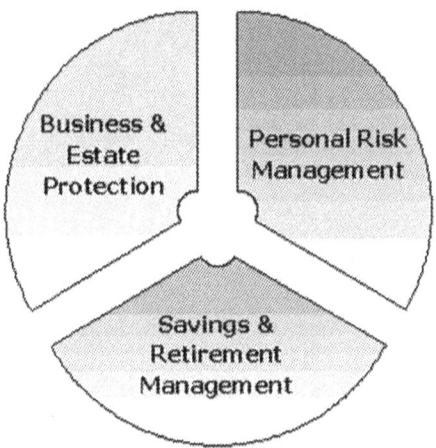

It has been three (3) full years since we chatted about those 'Personal Risk Management' issues. Guess what? Your life has changed in three years. Maybe not a lot, but believe me, you will notice a few changes. The fact that we just keep checking things over will give you the confidence to know that you can avoid crisis in your financial and insurance life by continually adjusting. Adjusting a little at a time has a whole bunch of merit in my book. That's why this system works so well. It's balanced.

"Balance is dynamic, ever moving, ever changing. Think of a tightrope walker holding a balance pole. One moment it's steady, the next moment it swings wildly to the right. Then it dips violently to the left. Then it's steady again. There is no 'right' place for the pole to be—the only 'right' thing to do is stay on the tightrope.

John-Roger & Peter McWilliams, 'Wealth 101—Getting What You Want—Enjoying What You've Got', Prelude Press

---

Challenge Questions

When I achieve my goals, how will that make me feel?

_____

_____

Who can help me achieve my goals?

_____

_____

How can they help me achieve my goals?

_____

_____

Minimums and Maximums

> "To be what you are and to become what you are capable of
> Becoming is the secret of a happy life."
>> Og Mandino
>> The Greatest Success In The World
>> Bantam Books,
>> page 93.

What happens when you put the least amount of effort into something? Think of your marriage or your career or your spiritual life or your relationship with others or your financial planning. What happens when you put the least amount of effort into those aspects of your life?

Wouldn't you think that the smaller amount of effort you put in to something, the smaller result you'll get going out? I sure do.

Some people have fantastic memories. They are said to have good recall. Good recall is simply the result of committing something to memory; that is, making a single-minded effort to connect with it, to link it somehow to something else. Then, you simply visit it often on a regular basis. Pretty soon...bingo! You have good recall!

A good financial plan and a good solid retirement is exactly the same thing. It takes single-minded effort to establish your own goals and objectives, you visit it and update it often. You nurture it. Pretty soon…bingo! You have a good, solid retirement plan!

In the book 'The Millionaire Next Door", the authors charted how much time the average 'middle income' millionaire spent planning their investment decisions. They spent an average of only 8.4 hours per month. That may not sound like a lot of time; however, those 8.4 hours per month was twice as much as their non-millionaire, middle-income counterparts. Do you think that 8 or 9 hours every month is a lot of time?

Although the time spent on planning investment decisions is not the only distinction between being a millionaire or not. It is simply one of the necessary criteria to become a millionaire.

Becoming wealthy may not be your primary focus. Owning your own company or working for yourself may not be your goal. But being financially comfortable and not worrying about bills all the time just might be a goal of yours.

One of the gigantic ironies of all time is that we are living in a period of human history that is unparalleled in financial opportunity. We are surrounded by opportunity, but many are living on the brink of poverty. So what's the problem?

According to the Social Security Administration's Office of Research and Statistics, for every 100 U.S. citizens age 25, here's what's happened to them by the time they reach age 65:

16	Are Dead
66	Are Dependent on the government or someone else
18	Are Financially Independent
100	Total

'Financially independent' is defined as income of more than $30,000 per year, according to the Social Security Administration.

I believe the problem is that we have too many toys, too little financial discipline and we're not nearly as goal oriented, as we should be.

When clients get focused, or re-focused on an exciting goal, something worth their time and effort, something that can generate an internal enthusiasm within themselves, they can achieve ANYTHING! It's been said that you need a 'burning desire' within you to keep you going through the times when things don't go so well. You must keep on track...your track for success, whatever you define success to be.

A trusted advisor can help immeasurably in helping you to see around a corner you've never seen before.

What would you try to accomplish if you knew you could not fail? What heights could you reach if you had no limits? Earl Nightingale, the infamous motivator, said many times, 'We are what we think about'. Whatever we think about, we become. Whatever we practice, we get better at. Whatever your goal is, you will probably achieve.

If there are no worthwhile goals, nothing worthwhile will ever be achieved. I've heard the statement many times about a ship leaving a port. Every ship leaving a port has a destination. Without a destination and a compass, ships would drift aimlessly.

Choose your goals and objectives carefully. Don't drift aimlessly. Take thoughtful consideration to the future and what you can become in it. The future is an exciting place. It is the place where we are all heading.

"No more effort is required to aim high in life, to demand abundance and prosperity, than is required to accept misery and poverty."

Napoleon Hill, Think and Grow Rich, Fawcett Crest Books, page 40

Challenge Questions

What would I do if I knew I could not fail?

_____

_____

This is what I could use to help me achieve my financial goals:

_____

_____

What am I willing to change in my life that will enable me to achieve my financial goals?

_____

_____

Why would it be important for me to achieve my financial goals?

_____

_____

My Short Term
(This Year)
Challenge Goals

1. _____

2. _____

3. _____

4. _____

5. _____

My Long Term
(Five year)
Challenge Goals

1. _____

2. _____

3. _____

4. _____

5. _____

Software

I fondly remember my first computer in 1984. It was used to compute
insurance illustrations, to do some basic retirement planning numbers
and maybe a couple of other chores. It was portable and it had thumbwheels. Yes, I said 'thumbwheels'. There was a thumbwheel for every
numerical digit. If you were 29 years old, one thumbwheel would have
to be turned to '2' and the other thumbwheel would have to be turned
to '9'. If you were a female, a thumbwheel would be turned to a particular number. A male would require a different thumbwheel position.
After 10 minutes of getting all the thumbwheels lined up, you'd check
them again. Then you'd push the 'GO" button and it started cranking
out paper. This was a real hoot! Thankfully, we've progressed!

Now we have notebook computers that can do what every room size
computer could do ten years ago. Way back in 1973 I worked at the
Pentagon. I served there in the Navy for one year. While I was in the

Navy they really did have room size computers. They used large reels of magnetic tape to store data. I operated them but I needed a lot of supervision operating them. They were fascinating, and I still don't really understand how they did what they did. To tell you the truth, I don't understand my little notebook computer either; I just know how to make it work. Now THAT I know!

It seems as if every part of a person's life could have a computer software plan to it these days. I think that's just great. Just so we don't overdo it and get bogged down in nothing but computer solutions to our entire life. But if we need some assistance in a particular area, there generally is a software program that actually could help.

Financial planning and insurance planning have some sophisticated software. A multitude of firms specialize in a mind-numbing array of analysis and in presentations that can effectively express a particular point of view. I try to utilize appropriate software and make it simple.

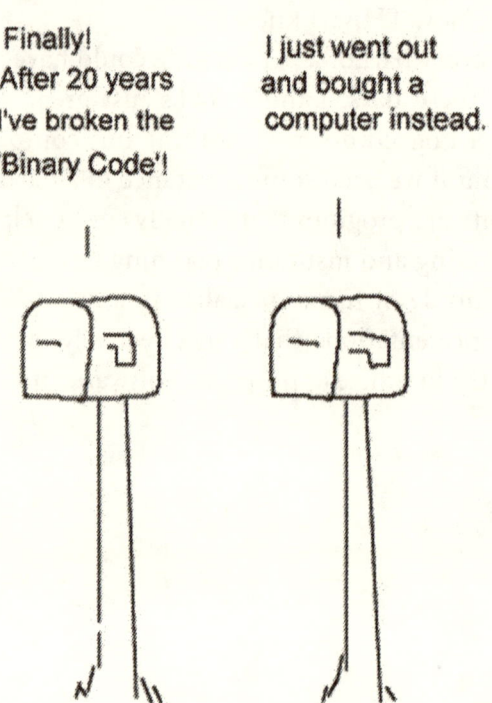

There are many ways to express those ideas and points of view. Financial and Insurance Planning software programs are constantly updated as soon as a new law passes and becomes a part of our everyday lives.

A portion of your annual review will nearly always include a computer software program to assist in doing the math as well as help in presenting a 'before' and 'after' scenario for you.

The perspective achieved by computer analysis is immeasurable when attempting to make a sound decision. If you can't understand the problem and the options, how can you make a good, sound decision? You don't want to be guessing.

Currently, I have four (4) separate financial and insurance planning software programs. However, the one that I use the most is 'Profiles +' a software program by Financial Profiles, Inc of Carlsbad, Ca. Many financial planners use this exact software across the country. This is state of the art stuff and is very comprehensive. Some of the areas that could be covered are:

- Investing
- Increasing your net worth
- Reducing the amount of taxes you pay
- Creating or improving your ability to outpace inflation
- Funding education and other goals
- Planning for your retirement
- Using insurance effectively
- Providing for a smooth distribution of your estate

Once you see this for yourself, you will appreciate it. It's very easy to understand. It's good. This software program is updated annually and is very well done. Having quality tools like this is similar to having a toolbox filled with pretty much every tool you could ever need. You don't use every tool every time, but when a particular tool is needed, I've got it for you.

As time goes on, expect improvements in computer software to help in meeting your goals as well as improvements in the way your goals and objectives are analyzed and presented to you. My commitment to you is to have current, up to date business tools.

It is also in your best interest, if you have it, to keep any printouts of any previous planning material. It helps when you look back and re-discover the criteria used which was made to formulate a basis for previous decisions.

Reasons To Get Started

If you haven't started with the 'Annual Client Review System' yet, there is no time like the present. Here are some reasons to do so:

1. To save some money
2. To acquire a greater awareness
3. Update your existing plan
4. Begin your own "plan"
5. Marriage
6. Initiate savings and investment programs
7. Ensure proper coverages
8. Divorce
9. Change of goals or objectives
10. Update beneficiaries on Life Insurance, IRAs, 401Ks, Annuities, etc
11. Review and update ownership of policies/plans/real estate/etc
12. Births in the family
13. A Death in the family
14. To discover what Settlement Options are available
15. Career Change

16. New outlook
17. New opportunities
18. Accomplished goal, need another
19. Retirement

20. All new lifestyle
21. Income issues
22. Protection issues
23. Change of investment goals

Reasons to get started...
... Let me count the ways!

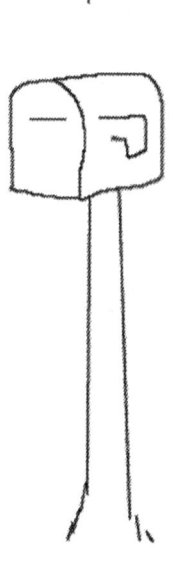

Challenge Questions

I would like to have my own personal reviews conducted at this frequency:

- ❑   Annually

- ❑   Semi-Annually

- ❑   Quarterly

Specialists

I'd like to chat with you about specialists. I have three thoughts regarding specialists: namely, no individual can know everything; there <u>are</u> specialists for everything; and finally, you must find a happy medium.

1.   No individual person can know everything.

For those of you who have tried this, you know why it will never work. One person that thought he knew everything was Archie Bunker. He wouldn't allow himself to reconsider his opinion of reality. As the world around him changed, he refused to realign his opinions. He was wrong in the first place and it got worse. He gradually found himself in stark contrast to the world around him and he became a joke. He was a laughing stock. The TV program had is funny moments, unfortunately, some people had, and still have, bigoted and prejudicial opinions of the world surrounding them.

To try to be your own specialist on everything will probably make you miserable. It won't work anyhow.

2.   There *are* specialists for everything.

Training has become specific and highly technical on as many topics as one can imagine. Specialists are available on a worldwide basis. As a Madison, Wisconsin elementary school experienced a mold problem; there was a 'Certified Industrial Hygienist' acting as a consultant to the school district. I didn't know until then that there was such a specialist, but you learn something every day.

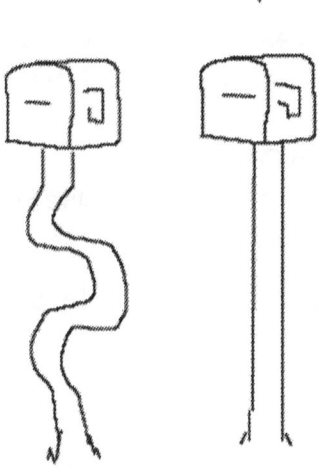

3.   You must find a happy medium.

You must strike a balance between depending on specialists and taking your own counsel. A good balance might be to regularly educate yourself on a variety of topics and also to count on trusted advisors who can act as specialists on specific topics.

"You're not sure when you engage in synergistic communication how things will work out or what the end will look like, but you do have an inward sense of excitement and security and adventure, believing that it will be significantly better than it was before."

Stephen R Covey
'The 7 Habits of Highly Effective People'
Simon & Schuster

Challenge Questions

How do I feel about 'Specialists'?

_____

_____

How could a Specialist have a positive impact on my financial life?

_____

_____

Who would be a Specialist I could feel comfortable and confident in?

_____

_____

I could use a little help finding qualified Specialists.

❏   Yes   ❏   No

Your Personal Advisor

"It is helpful to associate with people who are driven and focused on goals. They will help you stay focused as you travel the sometimes-rough path toward accomplishing your goal. They truly want to help you succeed."

Jeffrey B McMullen
Just In Time…Just Isn't Enough!
MG Publishing

Think of me as a personal advisor and an experienced professional insurance agent. Or you could think of me as a tour guide. You don't want a guide who has never made the trip before. If you need advice and guidance, you need advice and guidance not a passenger sitting in the back seat along for the ride.

As a personal advisor, and your life insurance agent, I'd have to say that a financial plan not reviewed or a policy un-serviced is very similar to a prescription for medicine that is open-ended and lasts for decades. That old prescription tries to cure a condition, which in all probability will either be getting worse or does not exist at all. This situation is simply not acceptable.

Have you ever bought a car and not serviced it? Even a family automobile needs to be serviced. A high performance sports car demands high performance service and attention. It requires much more attention than a relatively low maintenance family car.

There are many high performance life insurance policies too. Life insurance, annuities and investments are in use today that likewise require service and attention. Life insurance policies are contracts. These contracts are legal documents between the insurance company and you. Consequently, these contracts need to be reviewed and serviced on a regular basis, not just once every ten years or so on a haphazard basis.

Consistent, top-quality service is not a luxury, it's an expectation you deserve and should receive. As your agent, that is what I'm committed to do.

One of my commitments to myself, to my family and to my clients is to continually improve. To be able to improve means that I can provide a good life for my clients and my own family. One of the ways of accomplishing that is by reading. I have come to enjoy it. Reading has become one of my favorite pastimes. I read for the fun of it, I read for the spirituality of it, I read for the motivation of it and I read for the success of it.

During one of my reading adventures, I ran across William J O'Neil's book "24 Essential Lessons for Investment Success". In his book, O'Neil listed 'Ten Traits of Successful People'. This list hit me right between the eyes. Of the many successful people I have ever met, in retrospect, it seems that their predominant traits all seem to be among these. This is one of my all time favorite 'lists'! This could be a list of traits that you and I can work at diligently and achieve together.

"Ten Traits of Successful People

1. Positive thinking
2. Leaders make conscious decisions regarding what they're after, what they want.
3. Goals are nothing without action.
4. Successful people never stop learning.
5. Without a doubt, success is a result of being persistent and working hard.
6. Successful people learn to analyze details and seek out all the facts.
7. Focusing time and money is another key characteristic of success.
8. Success often means doing something differently, being innovative.
9. Successful people deal and communicate with others effectively.
10. Long-term success comes from integrity.

William J O'Neil
'24 Essential Lessons for Investment Success'
McGraw-Hill

Putting It All Together

This handbook was put together in order to give you some background as to how I work with my clients and the rationale for the way I proceed with my work with you. With your help, I intend to build a firm foundation for you in order that you may achieve your goals, whatever your goals may be.

One person who knows all there is to know about achieving goals is John Wooden. John Wooden was the legendary coach for UCLA and is considered to be the greatest basketball coach of all time. His teams won ten national NCAA championships in twelve years including seven national championships in a row. His lifetime winning percentage is over 80 percent! It is an unprecedented achievement in all sports.

In his latest book entitled 'Wooden', Mr Wooden said; *'You must be interested in finding the best way, not in having your own way.'* Taking this lesson to mind, I want to close with saying that it doesn't matter what I want for you, it's what <u>you</u> want to accomplish that counts; but together we can develop a plan that, when visited frequently, will place you right at the doorstep of <u>your</u> goals and dreams. That's the best way.

Challenge Questions

My personal financial advisor can help me in the following ways:

_____

_____

Ten years from now I want to be in the following financial shape:

_____

_____

I want to provide the following for my family:

1. _____

2. _____

3. _____

4. _____

5. _____

A Winner's Creed

If you think you are beaten, you are;
If you think you dare not, you don't
If you'd like to win, but think you can't,
It's almost a cinch you won't.

If you think you'll lose, you're lost;
For out in the world we find
Success begins with a person's will,
It's all in the state of mind.

Life's battles don't always go
To the stronger or faster hand;
But sooner or later the person who wins
Is the one who thinks 'I can."

Author Unknown

Challenge Questions

I am currently reading:

_____

_____

I am currently studying:

_____

_____

I am currently writing:

_____

_____

Putting It All Together

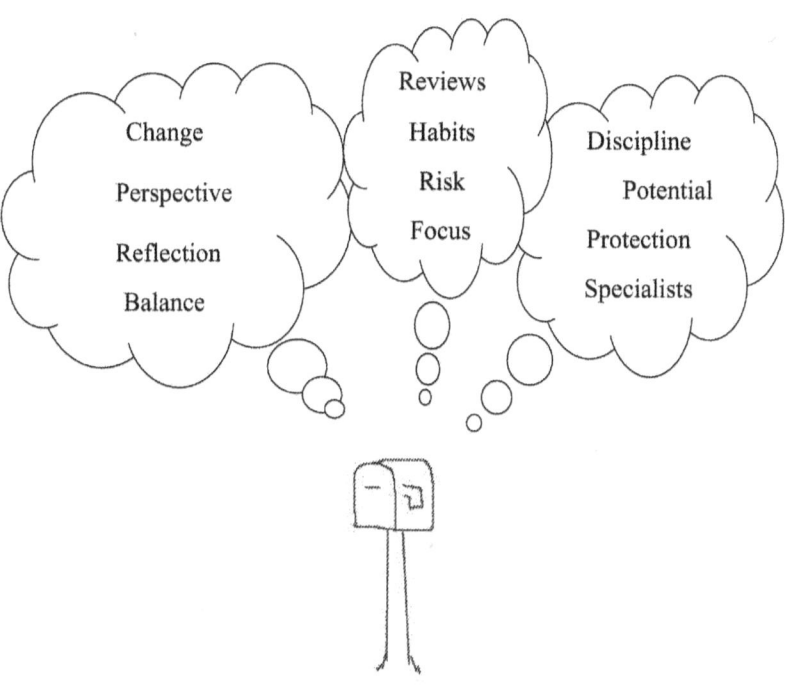

References and Acknowledgements

1. Covey, Stephen (The 7 habits of Highly Effective People) (Simon & Schuster)

2. Williams, Ellie (Investor's Desk Reference) (McGraw-Hill)

3. Berger, Esther M (Money Smart. Take The Fear Out of Financial Planning) (Simon & Schuster)

4. Fidelity Investments Institutional Services Company

5. Orman, Suze (The 9 Steps To Financial Freedom) (Crown publishers, Inc)

6. Altman, Alan W (Personal Empowerment) (Forest Publishing, page 149)

7. Chaffee, Roger B (This Week–23 Apr 67)

8. Rockefeller, Margaretta (Family Weekly–9 May 76)

9. Dyer, Dr Wayne (The Sky's the Limit) (Simon and Schuster, page 278)

10. Frost, Robert (The Road Not Taken) (The Poetry of Robert Frost) (Holt, Rinehart and Winston, page 105)

11. John-Roger & Peter McWilliams (Wealth 101-Getting What You Want–Enjoying What You've Got) (Prelude Press, page 49)

12. Mandino, Og (The Greatest Success In The World) (Bantam Books)

13. Hill, Napoleon (Think and Grow Rich) (Fawcett Crest Books, page 86)

14.Kiyosaki, Robert (Rich Dad, Poor Dad) (TechPress, Inc)

15.Tennant, Rich (Access 2000 For Windows For Dummies, 1999)

16.Steinfeld, Jake (Don't Quit) (Warner Books, 1993)

17.Lao Tzu, Tao Te Ching (The Tao of Leadership) (Bantam Books, page 141)

18.McMullen, Jeffrey B (Just In Time...Just Isn't Enough!) (MG Publishing)

19.O'Neil, William J. (24 Essential lessons for Investment Success) (McGraw-Hill)

About The Author

Karl N Kindschi, LUTCF, works as an Independent Insurance Agent and Registered Representative serving clients in south-central Wisconsin. He has served as Past President of the South Central Association of Insurance and Financial Advisors, has been the recipient of the National Quality Award, the National Sales Achievement Award and many other company recognitions.

Karl's responsibilities over the last 18 years have included being a Licensed Insurance Intermediary since 1984, a Registered Representative since 1986, a Registered Principal since 1996, a District Manager, an Advanced Marketing Specialist and Director of Life Sales, Training and Brokerage Sales.

Having authored and conducted 'Continuing Education Courses' and training conferences to insurance agents, Karl continues as an occasional guest speaker on insurance topics. He has conducted a variety of seminars and continues to speak at various public and community functions.

For more information regarding the products and services available from Karl N Kindschi, LUTCF, just call, email or write to:

Karl N Kindschi, LUTCF
PO Box 3
Portage, Wi 53901
Phone: 1-608-742-9934
Email: karlk@wisc-web.com

0-595-22254-4